Wait on the Lord

Wait on the Lord

Finding Faith, Growth, and Peace in Singleness

KYRA LANAE

GLORIOUS WORKS PUBLISHING
UPPER DARBY, PENNSYLVANIA

Copyright © 2025 Kyra Lanae
All rights reserved. This book or any portion thereof may not be reproduced or used in any manner whatsoever without the express written permission of the publisher except for the use of brief quotations in a book review or scholarly journal.

Unless otherwise indicated, all scripture taken from the New King James Version®. Copyright © 1982 by Thomas Nelson. Used by permission. All rights reserved. Scripture quotations marked (KJV) are taken from the KING JAMES VERSION (KJV): KING JAMES VERSION, public domain.

First Printing:2025

ISBN: 978-1-956196-04-7

Glorious Works Publishing
201 Bywood Ave. #2214
Upper Darby, PA19082
www.gloriousworkspublishing.com
Special discounts are available on bulk purchases. For details, contact publisher at admin@gloriousworkspublishing.com.

Glorious Works Publishing can bring authors to your live events. For more information or to book an event, contact Glorious Works Publishing at admin@gloriousworkspublishing.com or visit our website at www.gloriousworkspublishing.com.

Dedication

This book is dedicated to every person who has walked beside me in my journey of faith, growth, and peace in singleness, as I have learned to wait on the Lord.

With deep love and gratitude, I especially dedicate these pages to Cam, Bri, Mom, Mr. Gary, Nard, Tamika, Todd, Nees, T, Karla, Keacha, Kraig, Karen, and Ella. Your love, prayers, encouragement, patience, and presence are written into every chapter of this book.

Table of Contents

Introduction..1

Part 1: Identity and Foundation in Christ................................5
Chapter 1: Fully Loved, Valued, and Wanted..............................7
Chapter 2: Living with Purpose Now..13
Chapter 3: Christ Is My Provider and Savior............................19
Chapter 4: Purity and Obedience in the Waiting......................25
Chapter 5: Both Marriage and Singleness Point to Jesus..........31

Part 2: Surrender and Trust..37
Chapter 6: Trusting God's Good, Perfect Plan........................39
Chapter 7: Following God Moment by Moment......................45
Chapter 8: Don't Force What God Hasn't Ordained................51
Chapter 9: God Redeems Everything......................................57
Chapter 10: Trusting God with My Children and Future..........63

Part 3: Understanding Marriage and Singleness Biblically..........69
Chapter 11: Marriage Is Not the Prize....................................71
Chapter 12: Only Jesus Can Satisfy..77
Chapter 13: God's Design for Pursuit.....................................83
Chapter 14: Courtship with Purpose and Wisdom...................89
Chapter 15: More Than Compatibility....................................95
Chapter 16: Marriage Requires Sacrifice...............................101

Part 4: Heart Work and Healing..107
Chapter 17: God Reveals What's in My Heart.......................109
Chapter 18: Fear of Vulnerability and Exposure....................115
Chapter 19: The Comparison Trap..121
Chapter 20: Releasing Unhealthy Relationships....................127
Chapter 21: Surrendering Control of My Story......................133

Part 5: Walking Forward in Faith and Contentment................139
Chapter 22: Content and Surrendered...................................141
Chapter 23: Called to Singleness—Still Chosen, Still Blessed........147

About the Author..153

More Titles by Kyra Lanae..155

Introduction

On November 1, 2025, during my daily devotion with the Lord, I was prompted to reflect on a simple but searching question: What lessons have I learned, and how have I grown during my time of singleness that I might not have learned if I were married?

I began to list the different areas where I had seen growth in my life and character, along with lessons that I felt were worth sharing with others. One by one, I wrote them down and numbered them. By the time I finished, I had about twenty-five different items on my list. As I looked at what the Lord had shown me, I felt the nudge that I shouldn't just keep this to myself. I should share it. Not just with one person, but with many, in the form of a book. I felt a deep sense of joy at the thought of taking what God had taught me and offering it to as many people as He would allow.

Almost immediately, I was reminded of a book I had started writing in January of 2025 that I had put on pause. At the time, I thought it would be a book about my journey from singleness to marriage. But as you will find out while reading this book, I have yet to cross the threshold into marriage. As soon as I finished that list and knew it would become a book, the title came to me right away. It was the same title I had chosen back in January: Wait on the Lord.

Originally, the subtitle was When God Writes Your Love Story. As of December 2025, I don't know if God is planning to write a marital love story for me. But I do know the most beautiful love story that has ever been written, the one captured in the Bible and summarized in John 3:16. From that perfect love story, I am able to share how I have waited on the Lord and found faith, growth, and peace in singleness.

For God so loved the world that He gave His only begotten Son, that whoever believes in Him should not perish but have everlasting life.
John 3:16

On November 1st, I completed the outline and the first chapter of this book, flowing straight from my life experiences and my walk with the Lord. I told my kids, "I'm going to write a book today." They laughed at the idea of writing an entire book in one day. While I didn't finish it that day, the following Saturday, November 8th, I completed Chapters 2 through 23. In just two days, the Lord allowed me to pen the words you are about to read. I am truly grateful for the opportunity to be a vessel used for His glory and to serve other women.

I don't know if you are a woman who has been single your whole life, newly single, single for many years, single and longing for marriage, single and cautious about marriage, or not single at all and simply curious about what it looks like to wait on the Lord. But I challenge you, as you read this book, not just to read it casually. Take time to reflect. Use the space available to write down what the Lord brings to your heart and mind.

If you are married and know a single woman, I encourage you to gift this book to her. I will be doing the same with the first several copies I receive. Before publishing, I asked the Lord to show me women I could give this book to, and He did.

This book is a wonderful tool for personal devotion, but it may also bless you to gather a few close sisters or friends and walk through it together as you pray and read God's Word. Some topics may feel tender and intimate and best kept between you and the Lord, and that is okay. But there are also beautiful opportunities to share encouragement, gain wisdom, and grow together.

Whether you work through this book alone or with others, make it a special time with the Lord. Grab your favorite drink or a small treat and prepare to read, pray, laugh, cry, reflect, rest, hope, heal, release, repent, grow, and be strengthened. May you find faith, growth, and peace in singleness as you wait on the Lord.

<3 always,
Your Sister in Christ,
Kyra Lanae

*Wait on the LORD: be of good courage,
and he shall strengthen thine heart: wait, I say, on the LORD.*
Psalm 27:14 (KJV)

Part 1: Identity and Foundation in Christ

Chapter 1: Fully Loved, Valued, and Wanted

"The LORD has appeared of old to me, saying:
'Yes, I have loved you with an everlasting love;
Therefore with lovingkindness I have drawn you.'"
Jeremiah 31:3

I am loved, valuable, and wanted, even if no man ever marries me. This was what I came to realize with God's word is my foundation, Christ's sacrifice as my focal point, and with each rejection as a reminder to point my eyes to the one who loves me unconditionally. I remember vividly one night going through the cycle of feeling the pain and rejection, focusing on what Christ did for me on Calvary, and verbalizing that I am loved, wanted, and worth dying for. This came after feeling rejected by yet another man who initially seemed as if God may have been bringing us together. When it looked as if that door was closing, I began to repeatedly ask God with tear-filled eyes, "Why doesn't anyone want me?" The truth resounded in my heart loud and clear, the same truth that applies to every person who was ever created.

The evidence that we each are loved, valuable, and wanted is recorded in Romans 5:8, which states, "But God demonstrates His own love toward us, in that while we were still sinners, Christ died for us." Another truth that is widely known, or at least recognizable by Christians and non-Christians alike is "For God so loved the world that He gave His only begotten Son, that whoever believes in Him should not perish but have everlasting life" (John 3:16). Hearing that truth, believing that truth, and reminding yourself of that truth in the moment when you don't feel like anyone desires you are three separate things.

You may know and truly believe that you are valuable enough for Christ to lay his life down on the line for you, but at times, the circumstances of your life try to distract you from meditating and confessing that truth.

Remind yourself that you are valuable with or without a spouse. Your marital status does not complete you or define you. Colossians 2:9-10 (NLT) reminds us that, "For in Christ lives all the fullness of God in a human body. So you also are complete through your union with Christ, who is the head over every ruler and authority." Knowing that, how could we ever think that a human being choosing to marry us is more significant than the God of this universe clothing himself in flesh, for the explicit purpose of coming to Earth to die for us?

Years ago, I wrote a song to remind myself of what is true when I was starting to question my value based on my marital status. I wrote the song to encourage myself, but also to encourage any other women who felt the way that I was feeling, even if only for a moment. I challenge you to sing these words to encourage yourself and any other woman that you come across who believes the lie for a moment the marriage validates you.

He chose me,
He chose me.
He said, *"You're the one,*
I'll send My Son."
He chose you,
He chose you, too.
He said, *"You're the one,*
I'll send My Son."

Scriptures to Meditate on: Jeremiah 31:3, Romans 5:8, John 3:16, Colossians 2:9-10, Psalms 139:13-18, Jeremiah 31:3, Ephesians 2:10, Ephesians 1:4-6, Isaiah 43:1-4

How does knowing I'm loved and chosen by God reshape how I view singleness?

In what ways have I sought validation from others instead of resting in God's love?

_____
_____
_____
_____
_____
_____
_____
_____
_____
_____
_____
_____
_____
_____
_____
_____
_____
_____
_____
_____
_____
_____
_____
_____
_____
_____
_____
_____
_____
_____

Chapter 2: Living with Purpose Now

For we are His workmanship, created in Christ Jesus for good works, which God prepared beforehand that we should walk in them.
Ephesians 2:10

My life is significant now. Rather than waiting on marriage, which may never come, I'm choosing to wait on God. I'm waiting each day for His instruction and asking Him what He wants me to do. For years, it felt like I was preparing myself for marriage and constantly setting my gaze on marriage. It is a beautiful gift from God, but it's not the end-all be-all. I had to realize that my singleness is not just a waiting room for marriage.

It is very possible that I may remain unmarried for the rest of my life. And I don't want to waste my life focusing on something that may never be attainable for me. But there is one thing I know is always within reach: doing the will of the Lord each day of my life.

Maybe one day His will for me will include marriage, and maybe it won't. But my desire, and honestly, even my design, is to seek after God and pursue the purpose He has for me moment by moment.

Back in 2019, I wrote a book called *Pursuing Purpose*, where I looked at various areas of life to help readers identify God's purpose in each of those moments. Sometimes we think our purpose is one singular thing that God created us for. And yes, if we ever were to reduce our purpose to one main truth, it would be this: to know, love, and glorify God. But what I mean by "singular thing" is how we sometimes limit purpose to one assignment:

"Oh, my purpose is to serve in the children's ministry."

"Oh, my purpose is to be a business owner."

"Oh, my purpose is to start a women's ministry."

And while all of those may be things God calls us to, our purpose is not confined to one role or one season. Each day, He has a purpose for us. He has a purpose in *every single thing* He allows within that day. He has a purpose in planting you at your job, in your community, and in the family He has placed you in. He has a purpose even in the pain of your past and everything connected to it. And what about the passions He has given you? He has purpose in those, too.

So, whenever you feel tempted to believe that your life will have meaning once you become a wife, remind yourself of this truth: You were created on purpose, for a purpose, by a purposeful God. Your life has meaning today and every day, no matter what your marital status is.

Get into the habit of asking the Lord daily, *"What do You want me to do today?"* Ask God, *"How can I honor You and serve others today?"*

Scriptures to Meditate on: Ephesians 2:10, Romans 8: 28-29, Psalm 138:8, 1 Corinthians 10:31, Psalm 25:4-5, Deuteronomy 10:12, Galatians 5:13, Ecclesiastes 3:1-8

What are ways I can serve God and others in this season of life?

How can I shift my focus from waiting for marriage to waiting on the Lord daily?

Chapter 3: Christ Is My Provider and Savior

And my God shall supply all your need according to His riches in glory by Christ Jesus.
Philippians 4:19

As a single woman and a single mom, there were years when I remember thinking that if I were married, I wouldn't have to struggle financially the way I had been struggling. I remember imagining that getting a husband would be the thing that would finally secure me and my children financially.

It was like I knew God was my provider, but I still wanted the reassurance of someone on earth taking care of me and my kids. I had already seen God's faithfulness and His provision during a time when our family's weekly food budget was only $20. It wasn't $20 a day, or $20 a person, or $20 a meal. For myself and my two kids, it was $20 from Sunday to Saturday, for breakfast, lunch, and dinner.

I watched God's hand provide for us, so I had no reason to think that I couldn't survive on God's provision. I guess what I really wanted was to not have to trust God in that area anymore. I wanted to live in a place of comfort because I could see the consistency of a man's provision through a paycheck every week or every two weeks.

But one day, the Lord opened my eyes. He helped me see that I wasn't truly looking to Christ as my Savior in this area. Instead, I was looking for a man to come in and "save" me. But I don't need a savior other than the Savior, Jesus Christ, who I already have.

I have everything I need for life and godliness because of what Christ has done, and no man on earth could ever replicate that or take Christ's place. God supplies all my needs according to His riches in glory in Christ Jesus. And if one day the Lord, in His infinite wisdom, sees fit to give me to a man in marriage, I will recognize that my husband's resources are just resources. He is not the source. Christ is.

Whenever you feel tempted to think that a man will come in and save you in any area, emotionally, spiritually, or even financially, pause and remind yourself of the truth. Maybe you think a man will save you from loneliness, or that once he comes, he will point you to

Christ. And yes, husbands should point us to Christ, but if a husband never comes, you are not without hope.

You have Christ Himself, which is everything you need.

Scriptures to Meditate on: Philippians 4:19, Matthew 6:31-33, Psalm 23, 2 Corinthians 9:8, Acts 4:12, Colossians 2:9-10, Psalm 62:1-2

When do I feel most tempted to depend on people rather than God?

What testimonies show how God has provided for me in the past?

Chapter 4: Purity and Obedience in the Waiting

For this is the will of God, your sanctification: that you should abstain from sexual immorality;
1 Thessalonians 4:3

I can go without sex, and as long as I'm single, that is what God requires of me. In my book *Beauty for Ashes*, I wrote a chapter about sexual sin and my former addiction to sex. There was a time when I couldn't fathom how people went more than a few mere days without sex. My exception was for virgins, but for anyone who had ever opened that door, I never imagined it could be closed again.

There was also a time when I celebrated every milestone, first days, weeks, months, and then years of abstinence. At one point, purity was a major focal point of my life, and I wore it like a badge of honor. And while it is honorable, as the Lord has drawn me closer and closer to Himself over the years, it's something I no longer give much thought to.

Am I still human? Yes. Does God still allow me to experience human desires? Yes. But not only am I no longer bound by the sin of indulging in sexual immorality, it's not even something that regularly appears on my radar. Sometimes I'll pause and think, "Wow… it's been over twelve years since I decided to honor God with my body and save it for my husband only," if the Lord even chooses to give me away in marriage. But if I remain single for the rest of my life, my body still belongs to God. And even if I marry, my body will still belong to God first, and then to my husband.

I'm no longer waiting around for the day I will finally have sex again. I now see sex as a beautiful gift from God, designed to be enjoyed within marriage. There is a gift expressed in marriage that is not given to singles, but there is also a gift expressed in singleness that marriage does not offer: the gift of giving God your body completely.

You may be a single woman who has never had sex, and I commend you for saving yourself for marriage. I also understand that not everyone who is a virgin is so by choice, nor does being a virgin mean you have never struggled. Sometimes we create categories in our minds, those who are sexually immoral and those "perfect purity princesses" who have never had an impure thought or crossed a boundary. But over the years, many virgins have shared with me that even without intercourse, they have still crossed lines or dishonored God with their bodies.

Remember, sex outside of marriage is one avenue of dishonoring God sexually, but it is not the only one. What you lend your eyes, ears, mind, and body to can be sexually pure or impure.

Wherever your journey has taken you, I want to encourage you not to view purity, abstinence, and singleness as something to simply endure. Purity, abstinence, and singleness are areas where you can surrender everything to God. Surrender your body, but also surrender the desires He placed within you.

God established the only holy, safe, and honoring place for sexual expression. And if He does not open the door for you to express your sexual desires in the way He designed, then your call is to continue obeying Him, because obedience is the chief expression of our love for Him. Jesus said, "If you love Me, obey My commands."

When you don't have the means to express love through a sexual act with a husband, remember this:
You still have the means to express love to a holy God, through your obedience.

Scriptures to Meditate on: 1 Thessalonians 4:3-5, 1 Corinthians 6:18-20, Matthew 5:27-30, Ephesians 5:3, John 14:15, 1 John 5:3, Romans 12:1, Psalm 119:9

What boundaries help me walk in purity?

How can I view obedience as an act of love toward God?

Chapter 5: Both Marriage and Singleness Point to Jesus
…But each one has his own gift from God, one in this manner and another in that.
1 Corinthians 7:7

God has created two paths, marriage and singleness, and both are designed to point us to Jesus.

Early in my walk with the Lord, I remember writing down the question, "Why do I want a spouse?" My first response turned into a bulleted list: *companionship, to have someone to share thoughts, dreams, and ideas with, have someone who would motivate, encourage, and pray for me, and I for him, have someone I could give to, walk with, and help grow, and I desire to show God in my life.*

Over the years, my responses deepened. I began to write things like:

I want to display the relationship Jesus has with His Church by honoring and respecting my husband as he loves me unconditionally.
I want my submission to my husband to reflect the Church's submission to Christ.
I want to expand the kingdom by discipling as many children as the Lord blesses me with.
I want to love and serve my brother in Christ, my husband, in a way that shows the world I am a disciple of Jesus.

Earlier this year, my response shifted even more. It turned into this:

My desire is to love and obey (Deuteronomy 7:9), honor and glorify (1 Corinthians 10:31), please (Hebrews 11:6), and serve (Colossians 3:23-24) the Lord to the best of my ability. I understand and accept (Matthew 6:10) that if the Lord has me single for this season, or for a lifetime, it is the best way (Psalm 18:30) for me to do so (Hebrews 13:20-21).

Generally speaking, two are better than one (Ecclesiastes 4:9), but there are times when that's not the case (1 Corinthians 7:7-8, 32-35). If the Lord, in His infinite wisdom (Romans 11:33), has me single, then singleness is best for me. With my limited knowledge of the course of my life (James 4:13-15), I desire to be given to a husband (Matthew 22:30) so I can be a vivid expression of Jesus Christ and His bride, the Church (Ephesians 5:22-32).

I long to show the Church's submission to Christ through my submission and obedience to my husband (Ephesians 5:22-24). In a world sprinting away from God's Word, design, and order (Romans 1:21), I want to be a city on a hill (Matthew 5:14), declaring His design by my reverent lifestyle, first to God (Hebrews 12:28), and then to my husband (Ephesians 5:33). I want to live in such a way that my submission to God and my husband intrigues others (Matthew 5:16) and draws questions about why I live so counterculturally (Romans 12:2). I want my life to be a platform for sharing the gospel (Mark 16:15) and the relationship between Christ and His bride (Ephesians 5:22-32). And for those who are in Christ, my prayer is that it motivates them toward love, good works (Hebrews 10:24), and obedience to Christ (John 14:15), as they are reminded to lay down their own will (Galatians 5:13) and take up the will of another (Hebrews 10:36).

These desires overflow from my heart (Luke 6:45). But I am convinced that if God wills for me to serve Him in marriage, He will give me to a husband, and if not, He won't (Proverbs 16:9). Either way, my highest desire is to live in God's perfect will (Ephesians 5:17), loving, honoring, serving, pleasing, and obeying Him all the days of my life (John 4:34).

As my responses evolved over twelve years of singleness, I also began to realize something else: marriage isn't the only avenue that points to Christ or displays the beauty of life in Him.

As a single woman, I can draw near to Christ in ways, and serve Him in ways, that I couldn't if I were married. Paul teaches about the advantages of singleness, and the truth is this: both marriage and singleness are gifts. Both should draw us closer to Jesus and point others to Him.

So don't look at your marital status as something that prevents you from displaying God's design. You were created beautifully in His image, and He has enabled you to love Him and serve others in a way that a married woman, who must also care for the things of her husband, cannot. You can devote yourself more fully to Christ and glorify Him greatly in your singleness.

Scriptures to Meditate on: 1 Corinthians 7, Isaiah 56:3-5, Genesis 2:18, Proverbs 18:22, Hebrews 13:4, Colossians 3:23

When I think about marriage, what are my deepest motivations?

How can I celebrate both singleness and marriage as gifts from God?

Part 2: Surrender and Trust

Chapter 6: Trusting God's Good, Perfect Plan

Trust in the Lord with all your heart,
And lean not on your own understanding;
In all your ways acknowledge Him,
And He shall direct your paths.
Proverbs 3:5–6

God's plans are far greater than my own. Whenever I resist fully surrendering to what He is doing, my actions reveal that I don't completely trust Him or His good, acceptable, and perfect will. It is one thing to say with my mouth that I trust God, but when my actions contradict my words, it becomes clear where my trust truly lies.

Over the years, God has gently shown me the areas where I wasn't trusting Him. Whenever He allowed a gentleman to come into my life for a season, He would give me the opportunity to assess where my heart really was. When I believed God was bringing me and someone together, only for the situation to shift, I could see how tightly I was clinging to the possibility rather than clinging to Him. Instead of holding to what God was doing and not doing, allowing and not allowing, I was tightly grasping my own desires.

There were times when I saw a glimmer of hope and thought, "Finally, after all these years, the Lord is doing the very thing I've been praying for!" Then, when things didn't work out, I would cry out to God, "Why? Why are You doing this to me?" And each time, so gently and lovingly, the Lord reminded me: *Trust Me moment by moment. Don't get ahead of Me. Don't assume that because you trusted Me up to a certain point, you can now predict My next steps for you.*

You may find yourself in a similar position, trusting God up to a point, but then losing hope when things do not unfold the way you expected or prayed for. You might question whether God was even in it. The truth is, He may very well have been. But don't forget that God allows us to walk through trials to strengthen us and reveal what is happening in our hearts.

Surrender your desires to God. Surrender your will, your plans, your purpose, your hopes, everything! Let your surrender be full and without conditions.

Reflect on my adaptation of Betty Scott Stam's Prayer of Surrender:

> Lord, I give up all my plans and desires,
> all my purposes and hopes,
> and accept Your will for my life.
> I give myself, my life, my all utterly to You,
> to be Yours forever.
> Fill me and seal me with Your Holy Spirit.
> Use me as You will, send me where You will.
> Work out Your whole will in my life at any cost,
> now and forever.

Scriptures to Meditate on: Proverbs 3:5-6, Jeremiah 29:11, Romans 8:28-29, Isaiah 55:8-9, Psalm 32:8, Matthew 6:10, Luke 22:42, Psalm 46:10, Galatians 2:20

In what areas am I struggling to surrender control to God?

How can I show trust through obedience?

Chapter 7: Following God Moment by Moment
Your ears shall hear a word behind you, saying, "This is the way, walk in it,"
Whenever you turn to the right hand Or whenever you turn to the left.
Isaiah 30:21

God can lead me down a path toward a goal for the sake of the lessons learned along the way, rather than the goal itself. If He shifts my direction, it is never because He is fickle or unsure. It is because He wants me to trust Him moment by moment.

Earlier this year, I believed the Lord was leading me to write a book entitled Wait on the Lord. I began writing with the assumption that it would become a chronology of my journey from singleness into marriage with a particular young man. For six or seven months, I genuinely believed this was the direction God was taking me. During that season, He revealed Himself to me in extraordinary ways. I had no doubt the Lord was walking with me, confirming my intimate conversations with God through Scripture, through other believers, and through the gentle leading of His Spirit. It was a beautiful time, and I began marking pages in my journal that I planned to include in that book.

When the Lord made it clear that He was not ending my singleness through a marriage to this young man, I put the book on hold. I remember telling the Lord that I didn't want to write a book about "waiting on the Lord" while I was still single. Who would see me as credible? Who would believe my reflections on waiting for a love story when I had no love story to show?

But the Lord showed me that credibility does not come from my marital status, accomplishments, or circumstances. He is the One who chooses the vessel He wants to use. If He desires to use me in this season of singleness, then I must trust that He knows exactly what He is doing.

When the Lord placed it on my heart to write this current book, with the same title, Wait on the Lord, He shifted my perspective entirely. He helped me see that a change in direction does not mean He wasn't in it from the beginning. The lessons He taught me while I walked with Him, believing He was writing my love story, were the true goal, not the fulfillment of that story.

You may be able to look back on other areas of your life, maybe not writing a book or walking through a particular relationship, but in every area, God desires the same thing: that you trust Him moment by moment. He wants you to trust Him in every lesson, not become so fixated on the ending. The ultimate endpoint for us is eternity with Him. Everything else "under the sun" is an opportunity to learn, to grow, and to deepen our trust in Him.

Every experience, every disappointment, every redirection should lead us to trust Him more and more and more.

Scriptures to Meditate on: Isaiah 30:21, Psalm 119:105, Proverbs 3:5-6, Matthew 6:34, Psalm 37:23-24, Galatians 5:25, Matthew 6:33, James 1:4, Luke 9:23, Romans 5:3-5, Psalm 37:4-5, Proverbs 19:21

What lessons have God taught me through paths that didn't end the way I expected?

Where in my life am I tempted to focus more on the end result than on the lessons God is teaching me right now?

Chapter 8: Don't Force What God Hasn't Ordained
Rest in the LORD, and wait patiently for Him…
Psalm 37:7

If I try to make something happen, something will happen, but it will not ultimately be God's best for me. I know this truth all too well. While I write extensively about my singleness and my desire for marriage, the reality is that once upon a time, I was married.

For as long as I can remember, I have desired marriage. And I don't just mean since becoming a Christian or even since entering adulthood. From childhood, I remember wanting to be a wife and a mother. I wanted that so deeply that at sixteen years old, I was planning to marry my then–boyfriend. I ultimately married a different young man at nineteen.

I had known the man I married since I was fourteen. When we were boyfriend and girlfriend at fourteen, I remember feeling convicted that we shouldn't be together. I knew I needed to break up with him because First Corinthians says, "What fellowship has light with darkness?" and "Do not be equally yoked with unbelievers." Even though I wasn't faithfully walking with the Lord and had not fully surrendered my life to Him, I had surrendered pieces of my life to Him. I grew up in a Christian home and knew enough to recognize that because he had no desire for God, our relationship was not good for me.

From ages fourteen to seventeen, we remained friends while dating other people. When we eventually got back together at seventeen, I still knew it wasn't a healthy relationship. I wasn't necessarily thinking about being unequally yoked at that time, but there were other issues, namely, his refusal to be faithful. Not only were we dishonoring God through sex outside of marriage, but he repeatedly engaged in sex outside of our relationship.

We were caught in a cycle of his unfaithfulness and apology. After one instance, he proposed to me. My desire for marriage was so strong that I accepted his proposal even though I knew I shouldn't marry him. I knew so clearly that I shouldn't marry him that I ended up marrying him in secret.

During our engagement, we never discussed a wedding date. It was almost as if having the ring and the idea of marriage were enough. My family and friends knew we were engaged, but when it came time to actually get married, I married him on a random Friday afternoon with our one-year-old son as our witness, and only told my family afterward.

There it was. I finally had what I had longed for all my life. And it lasted all of six months before his continued infidelity ended our marriage.

Maybe you haven't tried to force a marriage like I did. But perhaps there is some other area where you have tried to make things happen on your own terms. Know this: there are consequences to forcing your own way. Sometimes you may even "get" the very thing you're striving for, but that doesn't mean it is God's will for you.

And for those who may be in a position similar to where I once was, trying to make a relationship or marriage happen, I implore you: let God have His way. Your outcome will be His ordained outcome in your life, whether that is with a husband or without one.

Scriptures to Meditate on: Psalm 37:7, Genesis 16, 1 Samuel 13:8-14, Isaiah 30:15, Isaiah 30:1-17, James 4:2-3, Proverbs 14:12, Matthew 6:33, Luke 9:23-24

In what areas of my life have I tried to make something happen in my own strength rather than waiting on God?

What relationships, desires, or plans may I be holding onto too tightly right now?

Chapter 9: God Redeems Everything

...To give them beauty for ashes, The oil of joy for mourning, The garment of praise for the spirit of heaviness...
Isaiah 61:3

God doesn't waste anything. He redeems my mistakes, both the ones I unknowingly make and the failures that come from my sinful flesh. How gracious and wonderful is our God!

If you've read any of my books, you know that I have made many mistakes. Some I walked into knowingly, some I didn't recognize until after the fact. One of my most notable mistakes years ago was being convinced that the Lord had shown me who my husband was, and I pursued him, for years. Yes, years! At the time, I had a warped understanding of faith. I believed that faith was simply intense hope: if I hoped enough for a specific outcome, then I had faith, and God had to make it happen.

Now I understand that faith in God is trusting that He is good, even when the outcome is not what I hoped for. It is believing that He will do good and that His ways are perfect, even when they don't line up with my prayers or requests.

During the height of this mistake, I not only believed that the Lord had revealed this man to me as my future husband, I actually told him, at the time, a professing atheist, that he was going to be my husband. Oh, the embarrassment when I realized he was not! Beyond the embarrassment, this mistake shook my faith. I began to question if I had ever truly heard God or even truly knew Him.

Yet, in God's sovereignty, this trial became pivotal in my Christian walk. It broke some of the false doctrines I had clung to and strengthened my understanding of God. Between my fleshly desires and His perfect sovereignty, God allowed me to walk through this journey to emerge stronger in faith and clearer in understanding how He operates.

Maybe your mistakes are visible to everyone, or maybe they are hidden deep in your heart. Maybe everyone sees a child born out of wedlock, an abusive relationship, or a public failure. Or maybe only

God sees what you did, or even how you think or feel about something in your heart. No matter what comes into your life, God doesn't waste it. He uses it for His glory and to make you more like Christ.

Romans 8:28-29 reminds us: "And we know that all things work together for good to those who love God, to those who are the called according to His purpose. For whom He foreknew, He also predestined to be conformed to the image of His Son." God redeems everything, shaping every mistake and every circumstance into His divine purpose.

Scriptures to Meditate on: Isaiah 61:3, Romans 8:28-29, Joel 1-2, 2 Corinthians 4:17-18, Isaiah 48, 1 Peter 5:10, Psalm 30:5

In what ways have your past mistakes strengthened your relationship with God or clarified your understanding of Him?

How can you remind yourself daily that God's sovereignty can turn mistakes into lessons and opportunities for growth?

Chapter 10: Trusting God with My Children and Future
I sought the LORD, and He heard me, And delivered me from all my fears.
Psalm 34:4

I can trust that if the Lord has a husband for me, he will be the man God has created me for and equipped to love my children. I don't have to fear that I will need to protect my children from my husband. As a single mom, after God, my children are my most precious treasure. All of their lives, I have been tasked with the responsibility of caring for and protecting them.

When I would think about the idea of marriage, sometimes the thought crossed my mind that perhaps I should stay single until my kids are grown. I had heard stories of step-parents abusing their stepchildren, and I didn't want my children to face that kind of hurt. While I knew that not every step-parent relationship ends in harm, the mere existence of those stories made me pause and question whether marriage was even a path I should pursue if God opened the door.

Over time, I came to the realization that if God has prepared a specific man to be my husband, He will also prepare him to love my children because of his love for God. I can trust the relationship my husband has with my children because I trust God. Every person in a blended family dynamic is loved and cared for by God. He has a purpose for each of us, and we are secure in Him.

If you are a single mom, know that you can rest safely in the hands of our Lord. You can also entrust the lives of your precious little ones to Him. My counsel to you is to wait on the husband that God has uniquely designed for you, because He has created him to be a husband to you and a father to your children.

And if you are a single woman without children, this specific message about trusting God with your children may not apply to you now. But hold on to this wisdom, because if God blesses your marriage with children in the future, you will still need to trust Him with your children through your husband.

Scriptures to Meditate on: Psalm 34:4, Psalm 112, Isaiah 41:10, Philippians 4:6-7, Jeremiah 29:11, Proverbs 3:5-6, Matthew 6:31-34,

Psalm 55:22, 1 Peter 5:7, Joshua 1:9, Psalm 127:1, Isaiah 54:13, Psalm 37:5, Deuteronomy 31:6, Psalm 121:7-8

What fears or concerns do you have about marriage and your children, and how can you surrender those fears to God?

How do you personally define trust in God when it comes to your family and future?

Part 3: Understanding Marriage and Singleness Biblically

Chapter 11: Marriage Is Not the Prize

…The unmarried woman cares about the things of the Lord, that she may be holy both in body and in spirit…
1 Corinthians 7:34

Marriage is not the prize. Both marriage and singleness are beautiful gifts from God that allow us to worship Him and serve others in unique ways. A sister of mine recently sent me a podcast episode on singleness and asked for my opinion. The episode was entitled *Redefining Singleness in the Church: An Interview with Dani Treweek* on the podcast series *Snacks and Good Company with Sherri Lynn*. The podcast focused on our view of community in light of eternity among brothers and sisters in Christ, whether married or single. While I didn't agree with everything shared, there were several points that reminded me of the beauty and purpose in both single and married life.

This school year, I have been working as a co-teacher with another first-grade teacher. This experience has allowed me to see the beauty and advantages of both singleness and marriage from a different perspective. When I had my own first-grade classroom, I had the freedom to lead it as I saw fit. I executed my responsibilities with diligence, love, and grace. Fast forward to this year: sharing a classroom with another teacher requires me to make room not just for my strengths and abilities, but also to accommodate hers and allow her to flourish. One of the benefits I immediately noticed was our opportunity to learn from one another and appreciate each other's strengths. Our current classroom does not look like either of our individual classrooms from last year, yet it is richer because of collaboration.

I often think of our co-teaching experience in terms of creating a video game character. When you build a character, you allocate limited points to different abilities, strength, speed, life replenishment, you cannot exceed the total points allowed. Similarly, in singleness, you might devote 55 points to personal devotion and 45 to serving others. But when God brings you together in marriage, your allocation shifts: personal devotion might decrease to 20, while patience and the ability to love without demanding your own way might increase to 40 each.

Revel in the freedom of singleness, the ability to wake up and spend hours in the Lord's presence uninterrupted. But also rejoice in the beauty of marriage: while your uninterrupted time may decrease, you gain the opportunity to love and serve your husband to God's glory. Embrace the season God has placed you in, whether single or married, for a season or a lifetime. Remember: knowing, loving, serving, and glorifying God for all eternity is the prize, and both marriage and singleness are beautiful ways to lead you to that end.

Scriptures to Meditate on: 1 Corinthians 7, 1 Corinthians 6:17, Psalm 73:23-28, Lamentations 3:24-25, Galatians 5:13

How do I view my current season of life as a gift from God?

In what ways can I use my season of singleness to devote more time to God and serving others?

Chapter 12: Only Jesus Can Satisfy

And Jesus said to them, "I am the bread of life. He who comes to Me shall never hunger, and he who believes in Me shall never thirst.
John 6:35

The purpose of marriage isn't to satisfy my every need, and no person on earth ever could. Only Jesus can do that. Looking back at the list I made years ago about why I wanted a spouse, I see now that I had expectations about the needs I believed a husband could meet. Some of those included companionship and someone to share my dreams with, and those aren't inherently wrong desires. But at times, I was tricked into thinking that every need I had could be fulfilled by a godly husband, and that's not true.

I tend to be an optimist and often envision the best-case scenario, imagining that things will always turn out perfectly. I remember discussing some of my frustrations with a close friend, admitting, "If I had a husband, he would stop me from making these mistakes. He'd put his foot down on the unwise choices I've pursued." As a single woman, the buck stops with me in most situations, outside of surrendering to God, of course.

My sister in Christ gently reminded me that even in marriage, that isn't necessarily true. She pointed out that I could be married to a husband who doesn't step up or correct foolishness, maybe due to passivity, maybe due to his own ignorance. And even with the best husband, I cannot assume that he will meet every need perfectly or manage life flawlessly.

Sometimes, we quietly believe in our hearts that marriage will solve all our loneliness or lack. Perhaps we think that happiness will automatically come from marriage. While marriage can bring joy, it does not prevent moments of sadness, frustration, or unmet expectations.

The only one truly equipped to satisfy every longing of your heart is Jesus Christ. Placing that expectation on any human being sets yourself up for disappointment and places undue pressure on your spouse. Remember: just like you, your husband is human, flawed, and susceptible to failure. Only Jesus is perfect, and only He can fully meet every need and desire of your heart.

Scriptures to Meditate on: John 6:35, Psalm 107:9, Psalm 63, Psalm 16, Colossians 2:9-10, John 15:4-7, James 4:8, Song of Solomon 2:16, Psalm 42:1-2, Revelation 3:20, Psalm 73:23-26, John 17:3, 1 John 1:3

In what areas of my life am I expecting a spouse or another person to meet needs that only Jesus can fulfill?

How can I deepen my intimacy with Christ today?

Chapter 13: God's Design for Pursuit
He who finds a wife finds a good thing, And obtains favor from the LORD.
Proverbs 18:22

I do not need to, nor should I, pursue a man. Doing so would be unbiblical and outside of God's design. One of the women God has used profoundly in shaping my understanding of biblical femininity and masculinity is Elizabeth Elliot. I am forever grateful to a sister in Christ who introduced me to her books, podcasts, and talks.

A few of Elizabeth Elliot's works that shaped my understanding of God's design for pursuit in marriage include *Let Me Be a Woman: Notes to My Daughter on the Meaning of Womanhood*, *The Mark of a Man: Following Christ's Example of Masculinity*, *Passion and Purity: Learning to Bring Your Love Life Under Christ's Control*, and *Quest for Love: True Stories of Passion* and *Purity*.

Some of her key insights include the concepts that masculinity involves initiation, while femininity involves response. In The Mark of a Man, she writes:

"People come with standard equipment—tongue, eyes, ears, hands, heart—which is usually provided for both men and women. But there is equipment which is radically differentiated: the reproductive system. Its functions are plain enough. Quite arguably, they are designed for initiation and reception. Is it unreasonable to probe deeper than the temporal function and recognize that these two are signs? May we not infer from them, as well as from creation's order, the meaning of masculinity—initiation; and femininity—response?"

Reading this, I was struck by the beauty of femininity. Elliot explains that what we see physically reflects what God designs spiritually. Romans 1:20 says, "For since the creation of the world His invisible attributes are clearly seen, being understood by the things that are made…" Viewing my physical body as a woman, as a picture of reception and response, reminds me that living in God's order is a beautiful reflection of His spiritual design.

When I step outside His order and pursue a man, I am no longer responding but initiating, which is contrary to God's design.

You may have heard someone encourage women to be "go-getters" or to "shoot their shot" in pursuit of a man. You may have heard men who misunderstand God's design suggest that a woman show interest by pursuing or being flirtatious. But a godly man will appreciate your femininity, your understanding of God's order, and your submission to it. He will operate within God's design to pursue you, just as God pursued Israel in the Old Testament and as Christ pursued His bride, the Church.

As Israel did not go looking for God (Ezekiel 16:8), and as the Church did not go looking for Jesus (John 15:16), as a woman you should not go looking for a man. It is his responsibility to find and pursue you. Do not allow desire or desperation to drive you to deviate from God's perfect design.

Scriptures to Meditate on: Genesis 2:18-24, Ruth 3:9-11, Ruth 4:9-10, Proverbs 18:22, Proverbs 31:10-11, Ephesians 5:25-28, 1 Peter 3:7, Matthew 19:5, John 15:13-16, Ezekiel 16, Romans 1:20

How might I counteract, with biblical truth, influences that have encouraged me to pursue outside of God's order?

What practical steps can I take to cultivate patience, trust, and faith in God's timing for relationships?

Chapter 14: Courtship with Purpose and Wisdom
…Unless the LORD builds the house, They labor in vain who build it…
Psalm 127:1

I don't need to date in the traditional sense the way the world, and even many Christians, often do. Instead, I desire to enter a courtship marked by intentionality and wisdom. About a year ago, I met a young man who seemed to have many of the qualities I would look for in a husband. Because I had not encountered anyone who made me think that way since coming to the Lord and growing in my understanding of Him, my first response was to go directly to God. I prayed, "Lord, how do I do this Your way?"

Before surrendering my life to Christ, I had been in multiple romantic relationships, but after coming to the Lord, I had really only been in one. There were a few brief moments where I spoke with someone for a day or two and quickly realized we were not compatible. Because of that, I had never truly given serious thought to how I should conduct myself when potentially walking toward marriage with someone.

That encounter, and the questions it stirred, became the springboard for several months of biblical study on marriage and how God brings a man and woman together. What stood out to me most as I walked through scripture was that I did not see examples of people "hanging out" for months or years to see if things might work out. Instead, I saw a consistent pattern: God presenting a woman to a man, families being involved, and decisions being made sooner rather than later, based on God's leading and the character of the individuals entering a God-honoring union.

I realized that rather than "testing out" men, I wanted to be led by God into a biblical courtship with marriage as the clear purpose from the beginning. I wanted intentionality, prayer, counsel, and the evidence of consistency between words and actions.

Modern dating often functions as two isolated individuals coming together. Only after things become serious do they introduce each other to their families. At that point, one of two things usually happens, most often the first. If the families see red flags, the couple either ignores them because they have already invested so much time and emotion, or in the less common scenario, they end things after months or years and find that emotional intimacy, if not more, was prematurely built.

My perspective is different. I want to involve those who love both me and the young man early on, because they can see things from perspectives we may overlook. If I begin to consider someone for courtship, my hope is that we would meet with my parents and seek their approval. I value their insight deeply. Above all, prayer and God's approval are paramount.

I encourage you to search the scriptures yourself and see how often you find the model of modern dating. If you want to see examples of God bringing couples together without dating, I recommend Quest for Love by Elisabeth Elliot. It contains over thirty real-life love stories. Before reading that book, I thought I was one of the few people who believed God could still bring a couple together without dating in the modern world. I later learned that many believers still take this approach today.

Scriptures to Meditate on: Psalm 127:1, Proverbs 4:7, James 1:5, Proverbs 13:20, Proverbs 15:22, 2 Corinthians 6:14, Proverbs 19:2, Song of Solomon 2:7, 1 Thessalonians 4:3-5

What boundaries and values will guide me if God leads me to courtship?

What fears or hesitations do I have about allowing God, not emotions or culture, to lead my relationship decisions?

Chapter 15: More Than Compatibility

But the fruit of the Spirit is love, joy, peace, patience, kindness, goodness, faithfulness, gentleness, and self-control.

When considering a husband, it's far less about shared interests or personality compatibility and far more about spiritual alignment and purpose. Recently, one of the men I thought might have potential for a biblical courtship asked me an insightful question that caused me to reflect on my only God-honoring relationship:

"In the past, what was one or more things that you found lacking in your relationships?"

I responded honestly:
Before surrendering to Christ in 2013, He was neither the foundation nor the center of my relationships. Christ was what was lacking.

After coming to Christ, I had only one romantic relationship, in 2015. In that relationship, Christ was at the center, but at the time, I believed we were so different that it strained both of us as we tried to meet in the middle. Now, ten years later, I understand something much more clearly: my husband and I will absolutely have differences, but what truly matters is that we share the same beliefs about Christ, the same commitment to following Him, the same conviction to keep God at the center of our marriage, and the same direction in terms of values and purpose.

It is easy to become wrapped up in superficial or temporal things that initially attract us to someone. The reality is that all of us will change. Everything from our looks, interests, hobbies, views on various matters, and even aspects of our temperament and personality will change as we grow to become more like Christ. The thing that attracted you to someone on day one or year one may be nowhere to be found in year five, fifteen, or fifty.

And let's be honest, has anyone truly decided to marry someone simply because they love going out to dinner as much as you do, or because they enjoy jazz like you, or because their favorite season is summer just like yours? I would hope not. And even if they did, that would never make for a firm foundation.

When considering a man for a husband, prioritize these things:

- He loves the Lord God with all his heart, soul, mind, and strength.

- He loves his neighbor as himself.

- He is committed to washing you with the water of the Word so that you may be blameless before Christ Jesus.

Am I saying it's wrong to desire shared interests or activities with your husband? Not at all. But those things should never be elevated above the qualities that create a firm foundation in marriage, qualities that will enrich your life in Christ and prepare you both for eternity.

Scriptures to Meditate on: Galatians 5:22-23, 1 Corinthians 13: 4-8, Romans 12:1-2, Micah 6:8, Matthew 5:16, Galatians 2:20, Colossians 3:12-14, John 13:34-35, Philippians 2:3-5, Matthew 22:37-40, James 1:22, 1 Peter 1:15-16, Matthew 5:44, Romans 12:10-13, 2 Corinthians 5:20, Titus 2:7-8, Luke 9:23, 1 John 2:3-6, Matthew 6:33, Ephesians 5:25-28, 1 Peter 3:7, 1 Timothy 3:2-7, Psalm 112:1-2, Proverbs 20:7, Joshua 24:15, Colossians 3:19, Jeremiah 17:9, Proverbs 14:12, Ecclesiastes 3:1-4, Proverbs 31:30, 1 John 2:15-17, James 1:14-15

What Scriptures anchor my definition of a godly husband?

How have my interests, habits, or personality changed over the years, and what does that reveal about the temporary nature of compatibility?

Chapter 16: Marriage Requires Sacrifice

... in lowliness of mind let each esteem others better than himself. Let each of you look out not only for his own interests, but also for the interests of others.
Philippians 2:3-4

If or when I accept a man's proposal of marriage, I am accepting a lifelong commitment to embrace continual opportunities to lay down my wants and desires for my husband. The life of Christ was a life marked by sacrifice, and as His followers, He calls us to that same path. Whether single or married, none of us escape the call to sacrificial living as Christians.

As a mom, and perhaps even more so as a single mom, I am no stranger to sacrificing for those I love. I have had seventeen years of experience, beginning with the sacrifice of my body during pregnancy, continuing through labor and birth, and extending into every season of parenting my two children. There have been countless moments when I've had to surrender and be selfless. A part of us may naturally lean toward sacrificing for those we love, yet there is always a threshold where our sinful nature rises up and wants its own way.

First Corinthians 13 reminds us that love does not demand its own way, and Titus 2 instructs older women to teach the younger women how to love their husbands and children. You would think loving your husband and children would be automatic, but when we consider the kind of love Scripture describes, patient, kind, selfless, and not insisting on its own way, we quickly realize how often demanding our own way contradicts the love God calls us to.

I remember my sister joking one day that I didn't have space for a husband. She was talking about the copious number of pillows on my bed. She laughed and said, "What if your husband says, 'I don't want all these pillows on the bed'?" We both laughed, but her comment made me think. As a single woman for most of my adult life, I have been completely free to decide how my home looks. Whether it's how many pillows I have or the layout of my space, those choices have been mine alone. While pillows and décor are small things in the grand scheme of sacrifice, they served as a reminder that even seemingly insignificant preferences may need to be laid down. Sacrifice often happens in the smallest of ways before it happens in larger ones.

Jesus gave us the perfect example of sacrifice when He laid down His life on the cross for all mankind. He surrendered His will for the Father's will. In the Garden of Gethsemane, He prayed, "If this cup can pass from Me… yet not My will, but Yours be done." That posture of surrender is the heart of sacrificial love.

In marriage, you may have desires, and you may express those desires to both your husband and to God, but be prepared to lay down your will for the will of another. This will be an ongoing act of love throughout your marriage and, truly, throughout the entirety of your life on earth as a follower of Christ.

Scriptures to Meditate on: Philippians 2:3-8, Ephesians 5:25-28, John 15:13, Colossians 3:19, Romans 12:1, 1 John 3:16, 1 Corinthians 13:4-8, Genesis 2:24, 1 Peter 3:7, Ecclesiastes 4:9-12

How does Christ's example of surrendering His will to the Father shape my understanding of what sacrificial love looks like in marriage?

What areas in my life do I tend to "demand my own way" and how might God be calling me to lay those down?

Part 4: Heart Work and Healing

Chapter 17: God Reveals What's in My Heart
"The heart is deceitful above all things, And desperately wicked; Who can know it?
Jeremiah 17:9

My heart is desperately wicked, and over time, the Lord shows me what's in it, even when I try to suppress the socially or biblically unacceptable behaviors that stem from it. Over the past twelve years of singleness, I have witnessed growth and maturity in my walk with the Lord, and I have experienced His grace as He lovingly points out areas that are not in line with His Word.

Recently, one area of my heart that the Lord exposed was the desperation I carried. Over the years, I had learned how to hide the outward appearance of desperation for a husband. It's common for women to be cautioned against showing desperation for a man. Desperation often carries negative connotations, and Proverbs reminds us, "To a hungry man, every bitter thing is sweet." If we lack something desperately, even a poor representation of that thing can seem desirable, but in reality, it is not truly sweet.

I had learned not to chase after men overtly, but subtle hints of desperation still leaked out over time. At times, it appeared in my eagerness to communicate with a man I was getting to know, calling, texting, or keeping conversations going. What the Lord showed me, however, was that deep in my heart, I was still desperate for a godly relationship to succeed. Even when I didn't initiate contact, my heart would race with anxious hope whenever a relationship seemed promising. I would begin to plan a future with someone I barely knew, imagining what could be, before God had fully revealed His plan.

By the age of twenty-two, I had already been married, divorced, engaged to a second man, and then engaged to a third. At that time, I wasn't walking with the Lord. When I surrendered my life to Him at age twenty-three, I longed to pursue marriage in the way God designed. I desired a God-honoring marriage and believed that, as I walked with the Lord and obeyed His Word, I would be married to a godly man within a few years.

Fast forward twelve years: the journey of purity and seeking the Lord continues. Even now, when a godly man comes along and things seem promising, my heart still wants to race to the finish line, saying, "Finally! I did it God's way!" But that hasn't happened yet. The Lord revealed that, even if it's not visible to others, there are still hints of desperation in my heart.

Whenever it creeps up, I surrender that desperation to the Lord and ask Him to help me not to be anxious for anything, but instead, by prayer and supplication with thanksgiving, to let my requests be made known to Him. Then, His peace, which surpasses all understanding, will guard my heart and mind in Christ Jesus. I want to surrender every part of me to the Lord as He reveals areas of my heart. There is nothing I want to hold on to, trying to do things my own way.

As the Lord reveals your heart, which, as Proverbs says, is desperately wicked, give it to Him. Don't cling to anything, thinking that by holding on to your thoughts, behaviors, or desires, you will somehow secure God's best. Give Him your heart, fully and completely. God is gracious. He doesn't pull back the sheets and expose everything at once. He is loving, tender, and gentle, pointing to one area at a time, saying, "Look at this. I want you to give this to Me." And by giving it to Him, you don't have to do anything grand or dramatic. Simply surrender it and trust Him to work.

Scriptures to Meditate on: Jeremiah 17:9, Genesis 6:5, Mark 7:21-23, Romans 3:10-12, Ecclesiastes 9:3, Psalm 51:5, Proverbs 28:26, Titus 3:3, Matthew 15:18-19, Romans 7:18, Psalm 14:2-3

What areas of my heart do I feel God has gently been revealing to me recently?

How do I typically respond when God points out attitudes, desires, or behaviors in my heart that I need to surrender?

Chapter 18: Fear of Vulnerability and Exposure
Whenever I am afraid,
I will trust in You.
Psalm 56:3-4

I've desired marriage for as long as I can remember, and although I was previously married, even until recently, I still carried a deep fear of being completely open and exposed before another person. A part of me wanted to keep my secrets and insecurities tucked safely away.

Years ago, I was in a romantic relationship with a young man I trusted deeply. I shared so much of myself with him, more than I had ever shared with anyone. Then one day, he posted private information about me on social media. He didn't mention my name, but anyone who knew our relationship could easily infer that he was talking about me. I was devastated when I saw those posts, especially because it happened around the same time I discovered he was cheating on me.

The betrayal, the hurt, the embarrassment, it all hit me at once. I already knew by his behavior that he didn't care for me the way I cared for him, but I never expected him to publicly ridicule me. That experience planted a fear in my heart that followed me for years.

At one point in my walk with the Lord, I noticed a pattern: anytime a relationship didn't blossom, I would let out a deep sigh of relief and think, "Good. Now I can keep my secrets and insecurities to myself. I don't have to expose anything." There were still parts of myself I was uncomfortable with, things I preferred to deal with privately. The idea of having a husband who would see me naked, physically and emotionally, frightened me. I wondered, "What if he exposes me like the other man did? What if he humiliates me?"

I had to surrender that fear to the Lord.

Do I still have things I don't want the whole world to know? Absolutely. But I have surrendered the fear of vulnerability before my future husband to the Lord. I believe that if the Lord gives me to a husband, it will be to a man who cherishes and cares for me. And even then, my ultimate security is in Jesus Christ, who never fails. So, if for any reason, my husband fails me, my trust will still rest safely in the Lord.

I know you have things about yourself that feel safe only between you and God. But I challenge you to trust Him completely with everything, even your insecurities. Trust that the person He prepares you for, if He does give you to a husband, will be a safe place for your heart. But more importantly, rest securely in the arms of our Lord and Savior, Jesus Christ. He is your true refuge.

Scriptures to Meditate on: Psalm 56:3-4, Isaiah 41:10, 2 Timothy 1:7, Psalm 34:4, Proverbs 3:5-6, Psalm 27:1, 1 Peter 5:7, Joshua 1:9, Psalm 23:4

How have past experiences shaped my fears in relationships?

What are specific insecurities I need to bring to God in prayer right now?

Chapter 19: The Comparison Trap
For where envy and self-seeking exist, confusion and every evil thing are there.
James 3:16

There were times when I compared myself to other married women, wondering, "How come she gets to be married but not me?" Even though I knew from my own previous marriage, and from watching the marriages of others, that being married does not automatically mean someone is fulfilled or honoring God in their relationship, the comparison still crept in.

It was a shallow thing to think, but it was the truth of what was happening in my heart. Those thoughts stemmed from pride, jealousy, and envy, things that are not from God. I would recognize those feelings and repent, yet the fact that they continued to resurface meant it was something I needed to deal with honestly before the Lord.

It wasn't only women I compared myself to. If I saw a man whom, from my carnal perspective, I assumed wouldn't have many women interested in him, and yet he was married, I would think, "Wow, even he is married." Deep down it was as if I was saying, "Someone wants her, someone wants him… but nobody wants me?"

But the truth is that every person is valuable and made in the image of God. I have no place to look down on anyone as if I am more desirable or more worthy than they are.

On the flip side, everything that glitters isn't gold. There are many couples who are deeply unhappy in their marriages, yet pretend otherwise because marriage is often treated in society as a status symbol: Someone chose me. Someone committed their life to me. Because of that, what appears on the outside may not reflect what's happening in the heart.

At the end of the day, the only person you and I should compare ourselves to is Jesus Christ. Let Him be the standard. Let Him be the one you measure yourself against. His life, His character, His humility, His love, those are what shape us and anchor us. Everything else will only lead you into unnecessary striving or discouragement.

Scriptures to Meditate on: James 3:16, Galatians 6:4-5, 2 Corinthians 10:12, Romans 12:3, Proverbs 14:30, Philippians 2:3-4, Matthew 6:33-34, 2 Corinthians 3:18, Philippians 3:12-14, Hebrews 12:1-2

In what areas of my life do I feel most vulnerable to comparison?

How can I choose to compare myself only to Jesus Christ rather than to other people?

Chapter 20: Releasing Unhealthy Relationships
Do not be deceived: "Evil company corrupts good habits."
1 Corinthians 15:33

There were relationships with men that I needed to end, whether I remained single or not. In the past couple of years, the Lord helped me let go of connections that were unnecessary and no longer served the purpose of honoring Him.

One of those relationships was with a former fiancé. At the point when I needed to finally close that door, it had been about ten or eleven years since our engagement was broken off. Although we hadn't been romantically involved for over a decade, we maintained a business relationship for several years. Shortly before I closed the door completely, he expressed a desire to try again, more than ten years after we had ended things and after years of an amicable professional connection.

A part of me entertained the thought for a brief moment simply because it was familiar. He was familiar. We were only a couple of months from our wedding date when he ended the relationship, and familiarity can be a powerful pull. But when I thought back on what our relationship truly was, I knew it wasn't God-honoring. I had no desire to return to anything that could draw me away from my Lord.

When we were together, we both professed Christ and served in ministry, but we were not honoring God with our bodies. It was like we were living double lives, and I had no desire to go back into that type of situation. I explained to him that the woman I am now, more than ten years later, is completely different from the woman he knew. Back then, I was not fully surrendered to the Lord. I wanted Jesus as my Savior, but I still wanted to be the lord of my own life.

Another relationship I needed to end was a friendship with a man that began as a platonic connection. For a brief moment, we discussed the possibility of pursuing something romantic, but we mutually agreed not to and decided to remain friends. A few years into that friendship, earlier this year while I was studying biblical marriage, the Lord revealed to me that I had developed a level of emotional intimacy with him that was not beneficial. I realized I did not desire to give any part of myself, emotionally or physically, to any man unless he was my husband.

Since we both knew that a romantic relationship was not the direction God was leading us, I respectfully let him know that I needed to end our communication. Our conversations were infrequent, maybe once every three or four months, but when we did talk, we shared details we didn't need to share. It wasn't sinful, but it was personal in a way that wasn't necessary or wise for a single brother and sister in Christ.

You may feel that men and women should be able to maintain platonic friendships, but I believe clear boundaries need to be established among brothers and sisters in Christ. Assess the relationships you have in your life. If there are connections that are pulling you away from God's standards, His will, or the direction He is leading you, release them. It is always easier to pull someone down than to pull someone up.

And if you do maintain platonic relationships with men, I caution you to evaluate the depth of your emotional intimacy with someone who is not your husband. Let your future husband be the one who knows you fully in ways no other man does.

Scriptures to Meditate on: 1 Corinthians 15:33, Proverbs 13:20, Psalm 1:1, Proverbs 22:24–25, Ephesians 4:2–3

Which relationships might the Lord be prompting me to release or redefine?

How do I feel about the idea of my husband knowing me in ways no other man does, including emotionally, and what can I do to allow that?

Chapter 21: Surrendering Control of My Story

...in Your book they all were written,
The days fashioned for me,
When as yet there were none of them.
Psalm 139:16

My goal for marriage shouldn't be "starting over so that I can do it right," as if doing so would guarantee a particular outcome for my children. Because I had two children out of wedlock, I always carried a desire to one day be married, bring children into that marriage in a God-honoring way, and experience the joy of announcing a pregnancy without the shame I once felt for having children outside of God's design.

I remember when I was married and thought I was finally going to have a child within a marriage. My husband at the time and I were planning to have another baby together, and we were excited. However, due to health reasons, we had to put those plans on hold. Coincidentally, we ended our marriage before we could bring a child into it, but I still remember feeling hopeful that I was "doing it God's way" that time, even though I wasn't truly walking with the Lord. Being raised in a Christian home meant there were parts of me that wanted to honor God, but because I was still functioning as lord of my own life, there were plenty of things I wanted to do my way.

There was a space in my heart that longed to enter my next marriage with the hope of a "do over" to honor God with a godly husband, raise godly children, and imagine that everything would fall into place. At times, my optimistic mind likes to view life through rose-colored lenses. But I've learned that even if God blesses me with a husband and more children, I still have to depend on Him and trust His perfect plan for my life and for theirs.

I've come to understand that even if future children are raised in a two-parent home with parents who love the Lord deeply, it does not guarantee they will love the Lord the same way. It does not guarantee anything at all. Sometimes we think life works like a simple formula:

$A + B = C$, and if we do this and do that, then we will surely get the desired result.

There are only a few things in life that are that clear, and one of them is this: if you believe on the Lord Jesus Christ and surrender your life to Him, you will be saved and live with Him for eternity. But even honoring God in your decisions does not guarantee a specific earthly outcome. The Lord allows tests and trials throughout our lives, even as we obey Him. Ecclesiastes reminds us that from our perspective, some things appear to happen "by chance," but God has a purpose in all of it. The righteous experience both joys and sorrows, and the ungodly experience both joys and sorrows. Life is not divided neatly.

So when you are tempted to think you can control the outcome of your story, or your children's stories, remember this: God is the One in control, and you will live with far more peace, joy, and freedom when you surrender your story to Him.

Scriptures to Meditate on: Psalm 139:16, Jeremiah 1:5, Proverbs 20:24, Proverbs 16:9, Isaiah 46:10, Romans 8:28, Philippians 1:6, Psalm 37:23-24, Job 14:5, Ephesians 2:10, Proverbs 3:5-6, Psalm 37:5, Jeremiah 10:23, James 4:13-15, Luke 9:23, Romans 12:1-2, Psalm 127:1, Matthew 16:25, Isaiah 55:8-9

In what ways do I sometimes view life as a formula, believing that certain actions should guarantee certain results?

What truths from Scripture bring me peace when I am tempted to take control back into my own hands instead of trusting God with my story?

Part 5: Walking Forward in Faith and Contentment

Chapter 22: Content and Surrendered
...I have learned in whatever state I am, to be content...
Philippians 4:11

I can desire marriage while still surrendering it to God and being content in my singleness. As humans, we naturally drift toward extremes. We tend to be black or white, all or nothing, turning to the left or the right. Yet throughout Scripture, the Lord reminds us of the importance of balance. He is a God of justice and mercy, a God of love and wrath. He Himself embodies perfect balance, and He calls us to walk in that same steadiness.

During my twelve years of singleness, I often teetered between wanting to be married and, at other times, not wanting marriage at all. Believe it or not, there were seasons when my time with the Lord was so rich and intimate that I didn't want anything to disrupt it, including a husband. I knew that marriage would completely reshape what my devotional time looked like. There were days when I spent eight to twelve hours in the presence of the Lord. For some, that may sound far-fetched, extreme, or even unbelievable, but for me, between my deep desire for Him and the natural bend of my introverted personality, I could easily sit before Him, meditate on His Word, and study for hours without realizing how much time had passed.

During those seasons, the thought of trading that uninterrupted fellowship for the responsibilities of marriage would cause me to shrink back and think, maybe I don't actually want that. But over time, the Lord brought me to a place where I can desire marriage and still be fully content in my singleness. At the end of the day, I want only His will, nothing more, nothing less, and certainly nothing outside of it, even if stepping outside of it seems like the quickest path to fulfilling one of my heart's desires.

A few months ago, the Lord revealed something surprising to me: the deep longing for marriage that I had carried for most of my life was no longer there. It wasn't that I despised marriage or didn't want it anymore, but that the deep ache had lifted. Marriage remained a desire, one I would welcome if God chose to fulfill it, but if He didn't, I was still completely fulfilled in Him. And it wasn't something I said to make myself feel better; I genuinely felt that way, and I still do today.

You don't have to choose between wanting marriage or wanting singleness. You can choose to accept whatever gift God gives you and offer it back to Him. If you are married, glorify God in your marriage. If you are single, glorify God in your singleness. Let honoring Him and being content in Him be your aim. Scripture reminds us that godliness with contentment is great gain, and that truth remains the anchor for every season.

Scriptures to Meditate on: Philippians 4:11-13, Proverbs 30:8-9, Ecclesiastes 7:16-18, Hebrews 13:5, 1 Timothy 6:6-8, Proverbs 4:26-27, Romans 12:3, Galatians 5:22-23, Proverbs 25:16

In what ways do I see myself gravitating toward extremes rather than practicing balance in my walk with God?

How can I hold my desires loosely before God?

Chapter 23: Called to Singleness—Still Chosen, Still Blessed

Wait on the LORD: be of good courage, and he shall strengthen thine heart: wait, I say, on the LORD.
Psalm 27:14 (KJV)

I may have the characteristics and attributes of a godly wife, and yet God, in His infinite wisdom, may still call me to singleness for the rest of my life. Over the years, I have often viewed myself through this lens. When I would read Proverbs 18:22, which says, "He who finds a wife finds a good thing and obtains favor from the Lord," I would think about a man finding someone who is already a wife in her character, someone whose attributes reflect the nature of a godly woman.

I would evaluate myself and conclude that I do have many of those traits. Earlier this year, during a study on biblical marriage, I compiled scriptures and characteristics that describe a godly, biblical wife. At one point I found myself saying, "I think I exhibit these traits, but I don't want to measure myself by myself." So I invited those closest to me, my parents, siblings, children, elders and their wives, and close friends, to evaluate me according to the checklist I created based on the Word of God. Their responses, questions, challenges, and conversations gave me richer insight into what it means to be a wife. And while I may exhibit and express many of these traits, and I truly praise God for that, I also accept that the Lord may allow me to walk in those characteristics and still remain single.

God does not owe me a husband because I have a gentle and quiet spirit. He does not owe me marriage because I carry myself modestly or behave with honor. He is not obligated to make me someone's wife because I am industrious, desire to bear and raise children, or long to tend to a home.

My highest aim is to glorify God. Every one of those characteristics can glorify Him and bless others whether I am married or single. So do not view the traits of a godly wife as a checklist that, once completed, earns the reward of a husband. Let your life and character be shaped into the image and obedience of Christ, not because it will bring earthly rewards, but because it honors God.

Your greatest reward is not marriage; your greatest reward is Christ. Rejoice and be glad, for great is your reward in heaven!

Scriptures to Meditate on: Psalm 27:14, Galatians 5:22-23, 1 Corinthians 13: 4-8, Romans 12:1-2, Micah 6:8, Matthew 5:16, Galatians 2:20, Colossians 3:12-14, John 13:34-35, Philippians 2:3-5, Matthew 22:37-40, James 1:22, 1 Peter 1:15-16, Matthew 5:44, Romans 12:10-13, 2 Corinthians 5:20, Titus 2:7-8, Luke 9:23, 1 John 2:3-6, Matthew 6:33, Titus 2:1-5, 1 Peter 3:1-6, Proverbs 31:10-31, Proverbs, 12:4, Proverbs 19: 14, 1 Samuel 25:3, 1 Timothy 5:14, Ruth 1:6-18, 1Samuel 1:1-28

What qualities of a godly wife do I see in myself, and how might these qualities still glorify God outside of marriage?

How do I feel when I consider the possibility of lifelong singleness?

About the Author

The question of why Kyra Lanae does what she does is more important than the question of who she is. Kyra's relationship with Jesus Christ and desire to please her Father, God, is the driving force behind everything she does. Whether writing books, speaking publicly, mentoring or encouraging others in her daily life, her heart's desire is to help people. As for who she is, Kyra Lanae is a Christ-follower and mother.

Kyra Lanae is an internationally known author, publisher, and dynamic, inspirational, and authentic speaker who empowers women worldwide in the areas of identity, purpose, relationships, parenting, ministry, and writing. She is the author of multiple books including, Beauty for Ashes: The Transformation of my Life's Darkest Moments and Pursuing Purpose: 5 Keys to Fulfilling Your God-Given Purpose. Kyra is also the founder and president of Glorious Works Publishing.

Kyra delivers wisdom and practical application as she shares her successes and failures transparently. Kyra is wise beyond her years which enables her to relate to women of all ages from Gen Z to Baby Boomers. When she writes or speaks, you are sure to walk away with a new perspective, unearthed courage, or reasonable next steps. She is like a gold miner of the heart, digging up precious treasures in the women whom she addresses. As women's identities, mindsets, and lives are transformed, so are their families, ministries, careers, businesses, and communities. As Kyra pours strength into women, she motivates them to continue the cycle of strengthening other women. Women glean from the faith, hope, and love that Kyra exudes as she walks women through her journeys of overcoming rape, divorce, addictions, and suicidal thoughts, just to name a few, and pursuing her God-given purpose in life.

Kyra Lanae has had the honor of being featured in 31Wife in Training, an international Christian Women's magazine based out of Cape Town, South Africa. Kyra has also been a special guest and speaker on podcasts, radio, and for ministries and organizations including Gathering Connection Fellowship, Simplicity HealthStyle, and CareerGPS. Kyra's refreshing spirit, wisdom, influence, and contribution has opened the door for recurring invitations from every organization with whom she has partnered.

Kyra Lanae can be reached via email at admin@gloriousworkspublishing.com. For booking or book publishing consulting, please visit gloriousworkspublishing.com.

More Titles by Kyra Lanae

Beauty for Ashes: The Transformation of my Life's Darkest Moments

Pursuing Purpose: 5 Keys to Fulfilling Your God-Given Purpose

Pursuing Purpose: 5 Keys to Fulfilling Your God-Given Purpose Workbook

www.ingramcontent.com/pod-product-compliance
Lightning Source LLC
Chambersburg PA
CBHW050909160426
43194CB00011B/2337